W9-AQB-322

Date: 9/6/13

**J 598.97 OWE
Owen, Ruth,
Snowy owls /**

PALM BEACH COUNTY
LIBRARY SYSTEM
3650 SUMMIT BLVD.
WEST PALM BEACH, FL 33406

POLAR ANIMALS
LIFE IN THE FREEZER

SNOWY OWLS

by Ruth Owen

WINDMILL
BOOKS™

New York

Published in 2013 by Windmill Books, An Imprint of Rosen Publishing
29 East 21st Street, New York, NY 10010

Copyright © 2013 by Windmill Books, An Imprint of Rosen Publishing

All rights reserved. No part of this book may be reproduced in any form without permission in writing from the publisher, except by a reviewer.

Produced for Windmill by Ruby Tuesday Books Ltd
Editor for Ruby Tuesday Books Ltd: Mark J. Sachner
US Editor: Sara Antill
Designer: Emma Randall
Consultant: Tom Mason, Curator of Invertebrates and Birds, Toronto Zoo

Photo Credits:
Cover, 1, 4–5, 7, 8–9, 10–11, 12–13, 14 (top), 17 (top), 19 (bottom), 21, 25 (top left), 25 (top center), 25 (top right), 26, 28–29 © Shutterstock; 14 (bottom) © istockphoto; 15 © Alamy; 16–17 © Superstock; 18, 19 (top) © Dennis Paulson; 22–23, 25 (bottom), 27 © FLPA.

Publisher Cataloging Data

Owen, Ruth, 1967–
 Snowy owls / by Ruth Owen.
       p. cm. — (Polar animals—life in the freezer)
 Includes index.
Summary: This book describes the snowy owl including physical characteristics, habitat, food habits, and how they raise their young.
Contents: The hunter — The world of the snowy owl — Snowy owl habitat — Physical facts – Fabulous feathers — What's on the menu? — Sitting and waiting — Snowy owl pellets – Snowy owl romance — Eggs and chicks — The future for snowy owls.
 ISBN 978-1-4777-0223-9 (library binding) — ISBN 978-1-4777-0233-8 (pbk.) — ISBN 978-1-4777-0234-5 (6-pack)
1. Snowy owl—Juvenile literature   [1. Snowy owl   2. Owls   3. Polar animals]   1. Title
2013
598.9/7—dc23

Manufactured in the United States of America

CPSIA Compliance Information: Batch # BW13WM: For Further Information contact Windmill Books, New York, New York at 1-866-478-0556

CONTENTS

THE HUNTER

A pair of large, yellow eyes scans the snow-covered land. The eyes slowly blink and then fix on a small movement in the distance.

Scurrying over the white snow is a tiny, dark shape—a lemming. The little creature doesn't know it, but these are the last few seconds of its life.

From its perch on some rocks, a huge bird takes off, its yellow eyes fixed on its victim. As the bird flies low over the snow, its wings cast a wide shadow. Finally, the bird swoops down and grabs the lemming with its long **talons**.

The beautiful bird is a snowy owl. Like all **raptors**, or birds of prey, it is a **carnivore** with excellent hunting skills. The snowy owl swallows the lemming in a single gulp and then returns to its perch to keep watch for its next meal.

A snowy owl

Raptors are hunting birds, such as owls, eagles, hawks, and falcons, which use their talons to capture other animals. The word "raptor" means "to seize or grasp" in Latin.

Talons

A snowy owl swoops close to the ground to make a kill.

THE WORLD OF THE SNOWY OWL

Snowy owls live in the northernmost parts of North America, Europe, and Asia. They spend much of their lives in the **Arctic**, north of the **Arctic Circle**.

For most of the year, adult owls live solitary lives, moving from place to place hunting for food. In summer, males and females get together to **mate** and raise families on the rocky arctic **tundra**. In winter, some owls **migrate** south of the Arctic Circle. Some North American snowy owls, for example, spend winter in New England or around the Great Lakes.

WHERE SNOWY OWLS LIVE

The red parts of the map show the main areas where snowy owls live, and where they breed.

Every few winters, a large number of snowy owls will migrate from the Arctic to more southern parts of the world. Scientists believe that when one of these migrations happens, it is because there is not enough prey, such as lemmings, in the owls' northern homelands. Then the owls are forced to move south to search for food.

Some snowy owls have migrated from the Arctic to find food as far south as Texas and Florida!

SNOWY OWL HABITAT

The arctic tundra home of the snowy owl is one of the coldest and harshest places in the world.

For most of the year, the tundra is covered with snow and ice. Freezing winds blow and temperatures can drop to -40°F (-40°C). No trees with deep-growing roots can survive on the tundra because the land is covered with just 3 feet (1 m) of soil. Below the soil there is nothing but permanently frozen ground, called **permafrost**.

For just a few weeks in summer, the ice and snow melts. Then the tough low-growing plants that live on the tundra grow new shoots and flowers, and the tundra's wildlife, such as the snowy owl, have their young.

When snowy owls migrate south in winter, they look for open, treeless places that resemble their tundra home. Some owls spend the winter on the Great Plains. Others hunt on flat areas such as farm fields, **marshes**, sand dunes, and even airfields.

A snowy owl sitting on a telephone pole

Few people get to see snowy owls when they are in their arctic tundra habitat. When the owls move south, however, they can be spotted watching for prey perched on fence posts, telephone poles, and hay bales on farms.

Snowy owls are very large owls that can reach a height of up to 28 inches (71 cm).

An adult snowy owl can weigh between 3.5 and 6.5 pounds (1.6–3 kg). As is the case with most types of raptors, female snowy owls are generally larger and heavier than the males.

On average, snowy owls live for around nine years in the wild. They can live for much longer, however. In 1988, a snowy owl was captured and had a band put around its leg to identify it. In 2004, the same owl was captured again, which meant the bird was at least 16 years old!

The underside of a snowy owl in flight

Talons

Tail feathers

When a snowy owl takes flight and its wings are outstretched, its wingspan can be as long as 5.5 feet (1.7 m) from wing tip to wing tip!

FABULOUS FEATHERS

Snowy owls have extremely thick plumage, or feathers.

The owls' thick, feathery **insulation** helps to keep them warm in the freezing temperatures of the Arctic.

Young snowy owls have white feathers covered with black, brown, or gray speckles. Females retain this speckled pattern throughout their lives. As a male owl grows up, however, he loses the darker markings and he mainly grows pure white feathers.

A snowy owl's white feathers help **camouflage** it against the snow and ice. A female's speckled plumage helps her blend in with the plants and rocks of the summer tundra when she is sitting on her nest, which is made on the ground.

An adult female snowy owl

A snowy owl's legs and feet are covered with thick, white feathers to protect them from the cold.

An adult male snowy owl

Feathery legs and feet

A snowy owl's main food is small **mammals**. When the birds are on the arctic tundra, their favorite prey is lemmings.

During the winter, when snowy owls migrate south, they will hunt a variety of small animals that live in the places they visit. In addition to lemmings, snowy owls eat mice, voles, rabbits, hares, and squirrels. Occasionally, they may catch and eat fish. To catch a fish, an owl must use its talons to grab the fish as it swims close to the water's surface.

Ptarmigan

Lemming

An adult snowy owl will eat over 1,600 lemmings in a year. That's around three to five each day.

Sometimes snowy owls will catch and eat other birds such as ptarmigan, seabirds, or ducks, geese, and other waterfowl. Snowy owls are agile fliers, which means they are able to fly fast and change direction easily. Their flying abilities make it possible for them to catch small birds in flight.

A snowy owl eating a mouse

SITTING AND WAITING

Most owls are nocturnal, which means they are awake and hunting at night. Snowy owls are diurnal. This means they are active day and night. They usually hunt at dawn and dusk.

Snowy owls use a "sit and wait" strategy when they are hunting. They find a perch, such as rock on the tundra, that is slightly higher than the surrounding area. Then they use their excellent eyesight to scan the ground and search for prey to come into view.

Sometimes a snowy owl's prey is hidden under snow or plants. Then the owl locates its prey's position by using its superb sense of hearing to listen for the animal's movements.

Owls have the amazing ability to turn their heads 270 degrees, or three-quarters of the way around. This allows the owl to look for prey over a wide area simply by turning its head with no need for it to move its body.

When a prey animal comes into view, a snowy owl flies to the animal, cruising low over the ground, and snatches it up with its sharp talons.

This snowy owl has turned its head to look behind itself.

A snowy owl swoops in to snatch up a lemming from the snow-covered tundra.

SNOWY OWL PELLETS

Snowy owls swallow their prey whole. Digestive juices in their stomachs then break down the flesh they've eaten.

An owl's stomach cannot break down teeth, bones, fur, and feathers, however. Inside the owl, these indigestible pieces of its prey are compressed into fat, sausage-shaped pellets. Then, about 24 hours after eating, the owl regurgitates, or throws up, the pellets!

A snowy owl pellet

Bird scientists, called ornithologists, study owl pellets to find out what the bird has been eating. The pellets are soaked in water so they fall apart. Pieces of feather and fur float to the surface, while heavier items, such as bones, sink.

Then a scientist can catalog all the different bones in the pellet to find out which prey the owl has targeted.

This collection of animal bones was recovered from three snowy owl pellets.

An owl will usually regurgitate its pellets in a regular place where it perches. If scientists can find an owl's perch, they may be able to collect lots of pellets from the ground below.

SNOWY OWL ROMANCE

Snowy owls are **monogamous**, which means they stay with the same partner, or mate, throughout their lives. An owl pair spends most of the year apart, but meets up in summer to breed on the tundra.

The male owl chooses an area that will be the pair's **territory**. The female will make her nest in the territory, and the couple will hunt for food there.

Before the owls mate, the male puts on a display for the female. He flies into the air making powerful wing beats. He flies in an undulating way, smoothly gliding up and down as if flying over imaginary bumps. Then he descends to the ground. Finally, he turns his back to the female, lowers his head, and fans out his tail feathers on the ground.

If there are lots of lemmings available on the tundra, as many as five snowy owl pairs may have territories in an area of just 1 square mile (2.5 sq. km). In years when lemmings are scarce, however, the owls create territories that are much farther apart so that each pair has enough food.

Female owl

A pair of snowy owls

Male owl

21

EGGS AND CHICKS

After a snowy owl pair has mated, the female chooses where in the territory to make her nest.

She uses her talons to scrape a bowl-shaped hollow in the ground. Then she presses her body into the hollow to shape it. Sometimes a snowy owl pair will reuse a nest from a previous year.

When the female begins to lay her eggs, she lays an egg every other day. In total, a snowy owl usually lays between three and 11 eggs. Once the first egg is laid, the female sits on the nest to **incubate** the eggs. Keeping the eggs warm is essential to help the chicks inside develop.

Each snowy owl chick hatches about 32 days after its egg was laid. So a single snowy owl nest may be home to chicks that are two and three weeks old, and chicks that are just two to three days old.

While the female snowy owl is incubating her eggs or protecting the young chicks, the male owl brings her food so she doesn't have to leave the nest.

Snowy owl chick

Unhatched egg

DEFENDING THE NEST

Wolves, arctic foxes, and large birds, such as skuas, will steal eggs from a snowy owl's nest. They will also kill and eat owl chicks.

Snowy owls are not afraid of protecting their nest and young. They will even defend their family against large **predators** such as wolves. When a predator approaches the nest, the parent owls dive-bomb the intruder.

Sometimes one of the parents will distract the predator. The owl pretends that it has a broken wing. It flaps around clumsily on the ground, leading the predator away from the nest. The attacker thinks it is about to catch an easy meal and targets the parent bird. When the predator has been lured a safe distance from the eggs or young, the owl jumps up and dive-bombs its enemy, scaring the surprised animal away!

Having a snowy owl pair as neighbors can be good for other types of birds. Snow geese, for example, often nest in the same places as snowy owls. When a predator approaches the area and is scared away by the owls, the geese benefit from their neighbor's defensive behavior.

Snowy Owl Predators

Arctic fox

Skua

Wolf

From bringing their chicks lemmings to eat, to frightening away wolves and foxes, snowy owls are caring, protective parents.

Father snowy owl

Lemming

Chicks in nest

25

RAISING CHICKS

When snowy owl chicks first hatch, they cannot see, and their tiny bodies are covered with wet feathers. Within a few hours they have dried and become little balls of grayish-white fluff.

After about five days, the chicks' eyes open and they can see. The chicks quickly grow bigger, and their bodies are soon covered with gray, fluffy feathers.

A snowy owl chick

Fluffy, gray chick plumage

Adult feathers

Snowy owls make many different noises, from shriek-like, high-pitched whistles to low, powerful hoots that can be heard up to 7 miles (11 km) away.

Both parents bring the chicks food to eat. At first, prey is torn into small pieces so it can be fed to the chicks. Within weeks, however, the chicks are ready to eat whole lemmings and other small animals!

The parent owls continue to bring the chicks food until they are five to seven weeks old. Then the chicks are able to fly and can begin to hunt for themselves.

Parent snowy owl

A chick eating a lemming

THE FUTURE FOR SNOWY OWLS

At this moment in time, snowy owl numbers seem strong and the birds are not in danger.

The owls' superb senses and hunting skills allow them to find food even when their world is covered by snow and ice. When their preferred prey of lemmings becomes scarce, the resourceful birds travel to new areas and hunt for different types of mammals.

In addition to the birds' own survival skills, there are laws in place that forbid the shooting and trapping of snowy owls. Also, the arctic tundra, where they breed and raise their chicks, is far from cities, major roads, and other human disturbances.

For now, the future looks safe for these beautiful birds that were designed by nature to live in one of the toughest places on Earth and survive life in the freezer.

Scientists estimate that there are around 300,000 snowy owls living wild in the world.

GLOSSARY

Arctic (ARK-tik)
The northernmost area on Earth, which includes northern parts of Europe, Asia, and North America, the Arctic Ocean, the polar ice cap, and the North Pole.

Arctic Circle
(ARK-tik SIR-kul) One of the major imaginary circles, called circles of latitude, that divide maps and globes of the Earth into different regions. Everything north of the Arctic Circle is called the Arctic.

camouflage (KA-muh-flahj)
Hiding or blending into one's background. An animal's fur, feathers, skin color, or pattern can camouflage it against its background.

carnivore (KAHR-neh-vor)
An animal that eats only meat.

incubate (IN-kyoo-bayt)
To keep eggs warm so they hatch.

insulation
(in-suh-LAY-shun)
Material that keeps something warm.

mammal (MA-mul)
A warm-blooded animal that has a backbone and usually has hair, breathes air, and feeds milk to its young.

marsh (MARSH)
A wet area with soft ground and low-growing plants, usually on the edge of a lake, pond, river, or stream.

mate (MAYT)
An animal's partner that it produces young with. Also, when a male and female come together in order to have young.

migrate (MY-grayt)
To move to a new area for a period of time and then return. Animals may migrate to find food, to mate, or to avoid extreme weather.

monogamous
(muh-NAH-guh-mus)
Having one partner, or mate, for life.

permafrost (PUR-muh-frost)
A layer of soil below the surface that is always frozen.

predator (PREH-duh-ter)
An animal that hunts and kills other animals for food.

raptor (RAP-ter)
A carnivorous bird that hunts for prey and uses its claws, or talons, to catch its meal.

talon (TA-lun)
A claw on a raptor.

territory (TER-uh-tor-ee)
The area where an animal lives, finds its food, and finds partners for mating.

tundra (TUN-druh)
A rocky, treeless, boggy landscape of low-growing plants. Below the surface is a layer of permanently frozen soil called permafrost.

Websites

For web resources related to the subject of this book, go to: www.windmillbooks.com/weblinks and select this book's title.

READ MORE

Frost, Helen. *Snowy Owls*. Polar Animals. Mankato, MN: Capstone Press, 2007.

Landau, Elaine. *Snowy Owls: Hunters of the Snow and Ice*. Animals of the Snow and Ice. Berkeley Heights, NJ: Enslow Elementary, 2010.

Patrick, Roman. *Snowy Owls*. Animals That Live in the Tundra. New York: Gareth Stevens, 2011.

INDEX